MegaSkills® Moments For Teachers

How-To's for Building
Personal and Professional Effectiveness
for the Classroom and Beyond

by Dr. Dorothy Rich

NEA Professional Library
National Education Association
Washington, DC

Copyright © 1998 by Dorothy Rich Associates
First Printing: July 1998
10 9 8 7 6 5 4 3 2 1

All rights reserved. No part of this publication may be reproduced, stored in an information retrieval system, or transmitted in any form or by any means including electronic, mechanical, photocopying, recording, or otherwise without the prior written permission of the NEA Professional Library.

Note: The opinions expressed in this publication should not be construed as representing the policy or position of the National Education Association. Materials published by the NEA Professional Library are intended to be discussion documents for educators who are concerned with specialized interests of the profession.

MegaSkills is a registered trademark of Dorothy Rich.

Book Design: Karen Semanek

Library of Congress Cataloging-in-Publication Data

Rich, Dorothy
    MegaSkills moments for teachers : how-to's for building personal and professional effectiveness for the classroom and beyond / by Dorothy Rich.
         p.   cm.
    Includes bibliographical references
    ISBN 0-8106-2006-5 (pbk. : alk. paper)
    1. Teacher effectiveness—United States—Handbooks, manuals, etc.
2. Effective teaching—United States—Handbooks, manuals, etc.
I. Title.
LB1775.2.R53   1998
371.102—dc21   98-24154
                                                              CIP

Quick Contents Guide
MegaSkills Moments for Teachers

Introduction..7

Part One. Nurturing Ourselves and Solving Everyday Problems Using MegaSkills

Confidence...13
Motivation..31
Effort..49
Responsibility...67
Initiative...83
Perseverance..99

Part Two. Working with Others and Putting it All Together Using MegaSkills

Caring...115
Teamwork...131
Common Sense..147
Problem Solving...163
Focus..177

Part Three. Grading Ourselves

My MegaSkills Report Card...193

Acknowledgments

First of all, I want to thank the remarkable teachers and school employees across the nation who continue to not only inspire me, but also the children and families they work with everyday. Thanks also to NEA President Bob Chase and Executive Director Don Cameron, for the longtime support they have shown for the work of the Home and School Institute/MegaSkills Programs. Timothy Crawford of the NEA Professional Library, who helped spark the idea that led to this book, and Rachel Venzant and the other Home and School Institute staff who worked on this project, deserve my special thanks for their efforts that made this book possible.

I am grateful to Melissa Balog, Marcie Dianda, and Leona Hiraoka for their comments on the draft manuscript. And finally, my thanks to Harriett Stonehill, Director of the MegaSkills Education Center, Rachel Ayala, and to all the MegaSkills Field Associates, who share with me the joys and concerns of educators and families working to enable all our children to learn what it takes to succeed.

Contents

Introduction..7
   The Never-Ending Report Card..7
   Getting the Most from this Book..9

Part One. Nurturing Ourselves and Solving Everyday Problems Using MegaSkills

Chapter 1. Confidence..13
   Speaking Up at the Staff Meeting..15
   Getting Evaluated on the Job...19
   Competing for the Same Job..23
   Defusing Anger..27

Chapter 2. Motivation..31
   Building My Own Enthusiasm..33
   Getting to Reading..37
   Fighting Boredom...41
   Thinking Ahead..45

Chapter 3. Effort...49
   Too Many Papers..51
   Too Little Effort...55
   Too Much Effort..59
   Teaching is Hard Work..63

Chapter 4. Responsibility...67
   Sharing the Load..69
   Getting the Kids to Do Their Fair Share.......................................73
   Running to Keep Up..77

Chapter 5. Initiative..83
   Reaching Out to New People...85
   Getting the Attention I Deserve...89
   Taking the Risk of Losing..93

Chapter 6. Perseverance..99
   Please Call Back..101
   Who's Up? Who's Down?..105
   It's Me Again...109

Part Two. Working with Others and Putting it All Together Using MegaSkills

Chapter 7. Caring...115
    Teachers Need Care, Too...117
    Caring in the Classroom...121
    Understanding Each Other..125

Chapter 8. Teamwork..131
    Getting the Teaching Help I Need...............................133
    Getting Help from Students..137
    Sometimes It Takes Two Heads..................................141

Chapter 9. Common Sense...147
    Taking Charge of Feelings—My Own..........................149
    Taking Charge of Too Much Talking—My Own..........153
    Giving Myself Time...157

Chapter 10. Problem Solving...163
    When the Talking Has to Stop....................................165
    When the Griping Had to Stop...................................169
    When the Cheating Had to Stop..................................173

Chapter 11. Focus...177
    Getting Ready to Focus..179
    Coping, but with a Plan..183
    Moving Forward: One Step at a Time..........................187

Part Three. Grading Ourselves

Chapter 12. My MegaSkills Report Card................................193
    Grading Ourselves...195
    And Remember..198

About the Author..199
About MegaSkills and the Home and School Institute............200
Further Reading from the NEA Professional Library..............202

INTRODUCTION

THE NEVER-ENDING REPORT CARD
A Message from Dorothy Rich

When I first said the word "MegaSkills" over a decade ago, I said it in a whisper. I had formulated this word in my mind to identify the really important basics we all need to succeed:

Confidence:	feeling able to do it
Motivation:	wanting to do it
Effort:	being willing to work hard
Responsibility:	doing what's right
Initiative:	moving into action
Perseverance:	completing what you start
Caring:	showing concern for others
Teamwork:	working with others
Common Sense:	using good judgment
Problem Solving:	putting what you know and what you can do into action
Focus:	concentrating with a goal in mind

In developing the original MegaSkills Program, which was created to build children's achievement in school and beyond, I had not thought about how much adults would gain from MegaSkills. It was only through feedback from parents and teachers about themselves that I began to understand the value of MegaSkills for adults.

Teachers and parents reported changes in their own lives. They told me: "I have the confidence to give a speech because of MegaSkills." "I now know how to talk with my supervisor, to have more ambition in my own life." "I've grown to become the teacher and parent I want to be."

They discovered that everyday problems seemed to be more easily solved. They got the *initiative* to request the records from the central office that never seemed to get sent. They used more *common sense* when they worked with other adults. They showed *perseverance* to get phone calls returned. They practiced *problem solving* when someone cut into the line in the front of them. In short, they made MegaSkills work for them every day, in a variety of ways.

What does it take to be the best we can be? I say it's a sense of know-how about using our MegaSkills and making *MegaSkills moments* happen. That is what this book is about.

Getting the Most from this Book

The MegaSkills experiences in this book present typical predicaments. Each is introduced by a problem situations and followed by a MegaSkills Moment.*

> Problem Situations
> Painful dilemmas! Memories that burn!

MegaSkills Moments
Sweet surprises; everyday miracles

The situations are meant to be tried on for size. They may fit exactly or they may need some alterations to fit. What they provide are rehearsals, practice for the real thing, i.e., everyday problem moments that come up and the opportunities they present for personal growth and development.

Try to be as interactive as possible with the material in this book. Ask yourself: How similar or different are the situations from what happens in my life? Would I say or do that? How would I handle these problems and create my own MegaSkills moments?

---

*Note: Each chapter also contains personal message pages and idea sparkers, where you are encouraged to write reminders to yourself about using and building your own MegaSkills.

MegaSkills Moments for Teachers is the first MegaSkills book for educators' personal and professional development. It combines "wise" words and practical actions. It's a trip to the MegaSkills "gym"—to build and restore your MegaSkills muscles. It's designed to help you create success.

Our Longer Learning Life

To be successful, adults today have to be renewed. We need to be renewing ourselves, if not everyday, at least on a bunch of days.

There is extraordinary learning going on every day in all of our classrooms. You can use these experiences to build your professional and personal effectiveness. How to do that using the unique and powerful message of MegaSkills is what this little book delivers.

Treat yourself. Read this book. Get ideas. Be creative. Think of how you can make more MegaSkills Moments happen for you!

Part One
Nurturing Ourselves and Solving Everyday Problems Using MegaSkills

1. **Confidence:** feeling able to do it
2. **Motivation:** wanting to do it
3. **Effort:** being willing to work hard
4. **Responsibility:** doing what's right
5. **Initiative:** moving into action
6. **Perseverance:** completing what you start

1
CONFIDENCE
Feeling able to do it

*Confidence needs nurturing.
This is true for children and for their teachers also.*

The Problem
Speaking up at the staff meeting

Making presentations to adults makes me anxious. Although I have often thought about doing it, I have never spoken up at a faculty meeting. Usually it's the principals and the veterans doing all the talking.

confidence

confidence

MegaSkill Moment
Speaking up at the staff meeting

Yesterday, even though no one encouraged me, I raised my hand and gave my opinion. It made me feel terrific!

I reminded myself . . .

that even though I may feel shy or reticent, my students depend on me to speak up for them. I willed myself into action—for them. And it worked!

WHY GOOD THINGS HAPPEN...

Confidence is that all important belief in ourselves. It enables us to make good things happen and to bounce back when not-so-good things happen.

The Problem
Getting evaluated on the job

I'll be evaluated soon and it's making me nervous. I know what I'm doing. How can I show it?

confidence

confidence

MegaSkill Moment
Getting evaluated on the job

The principal observed my class the other day and said he was very impressed, especially with the pacing of my presentations.

Before the evaluation, . . .

confidence

I audiotaped a few sessions and listened hard. Then I used a video recorder and watched myself and the kids. What I saw wasn't the greatest. I observed and evaluated myself. I learned a lot. I made changes that helped make me shine.

BUILDING MY CONFIDENCE

Notes to Myself:
Here is one thing I have accomplished on my own recently in or out of school. It might be learning to fish, teaching a shy student, using a computer, working out a new lesson, cooking a new dish, or figuring out how to put together a piece of furniture.

_____

_____

_____

I need a sense of my own competence to gain the confidence I need and deserve.

The Problem
Competing for the same job

One of the other teachers and I both applied for the new department chair position. We were both good, deserving candidates for the job. She got it and I didn't. I'm feeling really down.

confidence

confidence

MegaSkill Moment
Competing for the same job

Even though I still feel disappointed, I wrote her a note congratulating her. The note let her know I am ready to work with her and that I know she will do a great job.

I asked myself:

confidence

"How would I have wanted her to react if I had gotten the new position?"
"Do I still want her as a friend?"
"Will we still be comfortable working together?"
"Will there be other opportunities?"

The answer came back "yes" on all counts. So, I took my own good advice and followed the Golden Rule.

RECOVERING MY CONFIDENCE

Confidence ebbs and flows like a river. It doesn't run at high tide all the time. There are days when we know we can manage whatever comes and there are others when just getting out of bed can seem a momentous step.

On those more difficult days, it's helpful to be able to think back to a time when something happened and you managed to overcome some obstacle. It can provide the strength to keep going on days when confidence is running low.

Notes to Myself:

_____

_____

_____

The Problem
Defusing Anger

A parent came in and angrily pounded my desk. He said: "My child says that you are not a good teacher."

My first reaction: "How can that be? I am a good teacher!"

Instead, I took a deep breath before I spoke.

confidence

MegaSkill Moment
Defusing anger

I gathered myself and said:

"I am glad you came in to see me. Let's see what we can learn about this together."

It takes confidence for teachers, especially new teachers, to talk to parents. I know that many parents blame teachers for everything that's wrong. I need to plan if I'm going to change harsh words into encouraging words.

I keep a file folder . . .

on every student. I throw in little, quick notes and I glance at these before a phone call home or at conference time. It enables me to respond to parents with specific comments about their child.

It gives me confidence and gives parents confidence in me, too.

confidence

ENCOURAGING WORDS TO REMEMBER

Energetic	Positive
Inspirational	Do It
Courageous	Creative
Encouraging	Curious

Enthusiastic

My Own Words to Remember About Confidence:

_____

_____

_____

2
MOTIVATION
Wanting to do it

*Motivation thrives on
encouragement. Encouragement is the
"charge" for the motivation battery inside of
both teachers and students.*

The Problem
Building my own enthusiasm

The students seem to be exuding boredom. I keep pulling them along, but it seems like an uphill climb for all of us.

motivation

motivation

MegaSkill Moment
Building my own enthusiasm

As I pondered my students' lack of enthusiasm, I thought: "What about me?" Sometimes I feel so tired, kind of stale. That's when I realized that my motivation carries over to the class. When I get enthusiastic, they feel it and show it.

I decided . . .

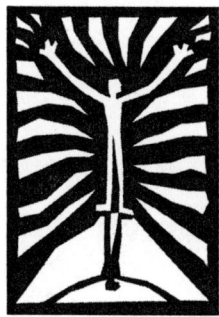

to share more of my own special interests (cooking, sports, gardening, for example). I linked these to what we're studying, including math and science. Pretty soon, the kids were sharing their interest and hobbies. The class really livened up for everyone.

Motivation, my own and the kids', builds on this enthusiasm.

MOTIVATING OURSELVES

Motivation builds when we feel important and involved. We can't always wait for others to involve us or to tell us we matter. We have to do this for ourselves. We make our own motivation.

The Problem
Getting to reading

motivation

We talk about the kids needing to read more. There are lots of days when I don't even get to read the newspaper, much less a book.

motivation

MegaSkill Moment
Getting to reading

I just have to make time for reading. Each day, I will take at least 15 minutes for my own reading. It might be a professional article, a news-magazine cover story, a chapter in a book, or even the advice column in the daily newspaper.

My students and I . . .

spend part of every class period, even just a few minutes, reading for pleasure. On some days, we will read aloud to each other. On others, we will read to ourselves. Afterwards, we'll take a few moments to talk about what we've read.

MOTIVATING EACH OTHER

Motivation builds on success.

I need to talk more about what the class is doing right, rather than what we may be doing wrong. I need to remember to take pride in what I'm doing and take pride in what my students are doing. I need to encourage them to do the same. This is how we can motivate each other.

The Problem
Fighting boredom

I get so tired of teaching the same stuff over and over. Whoever said that teachers don't get bored?

motivation

motivation

MegaSkill Moment
Fighting boredom

Reminder to myself: It's up to me to get "unbored." Nobody can do it but me. I have to do it myself. Even little things matter!

I decided . . .

that every morning before school, I'll look into the mirror and say to myself: "Here is one thing I am going to do differently today, one thing I am going to try in a new way."

motivation

BUILDING MY MOTIVATION

I am going to make a 30-second phone call to every parent of the kids in the class. I am going to tell them how proud I am of the class and one good thing that has happened. I'll ask them to share a good thing that has happened at home. They just might tell me what a good job I'm doing, too!

Notes to Myself:

_____

_____

_____

The Problem
Thinking ahead

When we feel caught in the daily routine, it's hard to look forward. I need ways to keep myself and the kids going.

motivation

motivation

MegaSkill Moment
Thinking ahead

To keep charged up, I try to envision the future and make positive predictions. I can almost see these kids grown up, doing well and remembering me as a great teacher. Giving myself this kind of support helps me everyday.

Each of us, . . .

my students and I, make predictions about the class and about anything special that might happen. We write our predictions on paper. They can be serious or silly. Each note is kept secret. We "bury" them and open them at the end of the year. It's almost a game, but it's a real motivation builder.

motivation

ENCOURAGING WORDS

Eager	Exciting
Go-getter	Internal Commitment
Push	Renewal
Urging	Visionary
Goals	

My Own Words to Remember About Motivation:

_____

_____

_____

3
EFFORT
Being willing to work hard

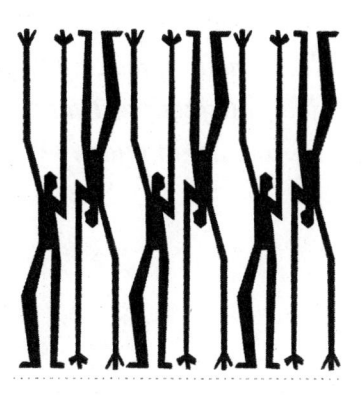

Effort not only gets things done, but it also has the added benefit of making us feel good. We feel satisfaction. That's the beauty of effort.

The Problem
Too many papers

When a batch of homework papers come in, I sometimes wish I hadn't assigned them. I just feel so overloaded.

effort

effort

MegaSkill Moment
Too many papers

When the kids asked if they could see each other's papers, I realized that while I need to review and grade some papers, I don't need to see them all. Also, a lot of learning can go on when students see each other's work, not to give grades, but to learn and to share.

Every week . . .

each student selects at least one assignment for me to review and other assignments for other students to review. We decide in advance which assignments qualify for teacher or student review. Then, we decide together on criteria for the review process. It's a great experience for the kids. Now they know what goes into grading.

EFFORT AND ENJOYMENT

Good teaching is a lot of work, a lot of laughs, and a lot of missteps. They only become mistakes when we don't try to fix them.

The Problem
Too little effort

I have too many kids in class who chronically ask me for help before they ever even try doing the assignment. It's frustrating to see my students fall into this habit. I wish they could learn to work more as a team.

effort

MegaSkill Moment
Too little effort

Today, I heard two of those kids, when they didn't know the answer right away, say to each other: "Let's look it up." I almost fainted.

I had told the class . . .

effort

to try hard to do the assignment—and to work together—before they asked for help from me. I could tell that some of the kids really didn't know that they could work together on many of their projects. After I told them, it seemed to release their cooperative energies with each other.

effort

BUILDING MY EFFORT

Working harder is not necessarily better. Working smarter is. My students need to know what goes into the job of teaching. I need to tell them.

I need to be ready in advance when children complain about school or about homework. I need to get across the message that I understand their concern, but that I have a job to do.

Notes to Myself:

_____

_____

_____

The Problem
Too much effort

Sometimes I over-prepare for a lesson. I worry every detail. It drives me crazy, and I get so nervous that I don't do all that well.

effort

MegaSkill Moment
Too much effort

Today, I prepared a new lesson, and I just knew . . . my preparation was just right, not too much and not too little.

I realized . . .

that I didn't have to know all the answers myself in advance. When I didn't know something, I'd say to the kids: "Let's look it up together." That way it's a shared effort, and not just mine alone.

WE GET STRENGTH FROM EACH OTHER

To accomplish a large task as a team, we divide the labor, and each of us goes off to do part of the task. That is the way we make dinner, run a household, manage a business, and—yes—teach our students.

The Problem
Teaching is hard work

effort

I dragged myself to school today. I was so tired. I thought I wasn't going to make it through the day.

effort

MegaSkill Moment
Teaching is hard work

A couple of students came up to me and asked how they could help. "Could we do some of the stuff you usually do all by yourself," they asked. I must have looked really dispirited, but also it was a lesson to me that maybe I have been doing too much all by myself.

Yesterday, the students and I talked . . .

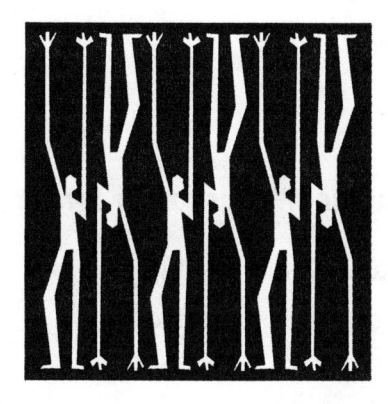

about how we spend our days. What we do when and where and how much time it takes. I told the kids about my schedule. They said, "Whew, we never knew you had to do all that!" It was eye-opening for them, and for me.

effort

ENCOURAGING WORDS ABOUT EFFORT

Hard Working   Painstaking
Resourceful   Effective
Diligent   Efficient

Reminder Words to Myself:

_____

_____

_____

4
RESPONSIBILITY
Doing what's right

*Doing it right means trying
to do right. It does not mean doing it all by
myself or getting it right all the time.*

The Problem
Sharing the load

responsibility

Goals for the new millennium. New curriculum standards. High-stakes assessments. It's all mounting up. I can't be responsible for children's achievement all by myself.

responsibility

MegaSkill Moment
Sharing the load

I can't be the only one knowing what we will be learning this year. I need parents on my side, working with and encouraging students.

Early in the school year . . .

I will send home a brief overview of what we're aiming to accomplish in my class this year. Letting parents know what's going on week by week is great, but helping them get a grasp of the whole year is equally important. I can't always be sure of praise when parents come to see me, but I want to be sure they I can answer "yes" to this question: "Have your students' parents received the information they need so they know what they can do to help?"

Everybody Seems To Be Busy These Days

Most of us need to be needed. We like being busy, feeling in tune with the rhythms of modern life—not running about and being strung out. We need responsibilities, but in manageable doses.

The Problem
Getting the kids to do their fair share

responsibility

My class is often still at work when the bell rings. The room is left in a major mess as the kids run to catch the bus or scurry to their next class. I'm left with the clearing up.

responsibility

MegaSkill Moment
Getting the kids to do their fair share

Today, as I looked around the classroom as the bell rang, I saw very little mess. I saw neatness and order and it was the kids who did it. Could this be a result of what I said to the kids yesterday?

Like many teachers, I was so pleased that my students were into their work that I tended to overlook how I felt.

Yesterday, for the first time . . .

I told the kids how overloaded and discouraged I felt when I faced the mess at the end of class. I asked them to put themselves in my place: "How would you feel?" Today, I could see the results. My continuing responsibility will be to help them keep it up.

GETTING ORGANIZED
TO MEET RESPONSIBILITIES

There is no magic formula to getting organized. Some of us love lists. Others do it with little notes scattered all over the office, all over the house. And some of us do it in our heads.

Don't agonize about whether to keep a piece of paper you need because some time-management guru from the '70s says "only touch a piece of paper once."

What works, works and it works differently for each of us.

The Problem
Running to keep up

responsibility

There is so much going on . . . I can barely figure out what I have to do. Some days I feel absolutely overwhelmed. Because I am so responsible, I feel that I have to do it all.

responsibility

MegaSkill Moment
Running to keep up

My realization: Not everything has to be done all at once. Some tasks are more important than others. Identifying priorities is vital for me. I need to find ways to keep myself on track . . . doing first things first.

I developed a simple tool:

I take a piece of paper and divide it into three columns—"Now," "Later," and "Never." In the *Now* column, I write any responsibilities that can't be put off, even till tomorrow. In the *Later* column, I put responsibilities that can wait. In the *Never* column, I put those responsibilities that I may not have to tackle, ever. I try to be very tough in making these decisions. It takes practice.

BUILDING MY RESPONSIBILITY

Some responsibilities loom so large, for teachers and students, that they seem almost impossible to get started on. From doing a term paper to moving to a new job to moving to a new town, large responsibilities provoke large anxiety.

The only answer for me is to begin, to start chipping away at the mountain, to make the initial moves that get me going. Once I get into motion, it's easier to stay in motion. This is both a law of physics and a law of human nature.

Notes to Myself:

_____

_____

_____

TAKE CHARGE

We all look for ways to be more in charge of our responsibilities, rather than having them be in charge of us.

One New Way for Me:

_____
_____
_____
_____
_____
_____
_____

The next page is left blank so you can continue your notes to yourself.

responsibility

5
INITIATIVE
Moving into action

*Ask a question you have
never asked before. Take an action you
have never taken before.*

*Small steps can be as vital
as big steps.*

The PROBLEM
Reaching out to new people

initiative

I was asked to represent the school at a meeting where I would know no one. I was supposed to meet, greet, and talk up what we were doing at our school. I kept starting conversations and getting abrupt one-word answers. My conversations were awkward and going nowhere.

initiative

MegaSkill Moment
Reaching out to new people

I soon began to get the hang of it. Instead of just asking, "Where are you from?" I would add words like, "I think I've heard of your school. I'd like to know more about it."

This seems like such a simple thing, but it made a big difference and gave me important insights for my classroom practice, too.

I listened . . .

and as I overhead more of these people talking, I began to understand what was happening. I had been initiating questions that elicited one word answers, "Yes" or "No." There was never any jumping off point for continuing the conversation. It was just like the classroom when the discussion would die. As I listened to others, I learned that I needed to ask the kinds of questions that kept the other person talking.

SHARING WITH A COLLEAGUE

It can get very lonely in the classroom with no other adults to talk to. I need to find time every day, even if for only for a few minutes, to talk with a colleague and to share something about what I am doing.

The Problem
Getting the attention I deserve

initiative

I get a feeling that my professional opinions are not sufficiently seriously considered. The teacher's voice can go unheard at the School Board meetings I go to. I often raise my hand and never get called on.

initiative

MegaSkill Moment
Getting the attention I deserve

There's an old saying that's still true: "The squeaky wheel gets the oil." My views are not always like other people's. So, maybe, I was being ignored on purpose. I felt a little uncomfortable and some might think I was calling attention to myself. But, I got up . . . and it worked.

Instead of letting the meeting end without getting called on . . .

initiative

I stood up and said that I wanted to say a few words. I had my say, which generated some useful discussion. I don't know how the others there felt about what I did, but I took the initiative and I felt proud of myself.

initiative

INNOVATE AND INITIATE

Mobilize the abilities of your students and their families. These days especially, there is a lot of expertise outside the classroom.

Start a *Teach the Teacher Day* at your school. Children and their parents present and share what they know and everyone benefits.

The Problem
Taking the risk of losing

initiative

I was asked to nominate a class in our school to enter a competition for a district award. There has always been one class getting every honor. I thought it was time to give another group a chance. I knew the risk—we could lose when we might have won.

initiative

MegaSkill Moment
Taking the risk of losing

I did take the risk and the prize was not awarded to our school. But, in losing, we really won.

The class that had never been chosen for anything finally got chosen for something. The kids were delighted. They worked intensively on their prize entry. They came together as a group. They tried hard and in trying, they won.

I was honest with my kids . . .

about why they were chosen. They understood that I took a risk and they felt proud of themselves for earning my trust.

My initiative on behalf of these students gave them a sense of pride and built more initiative. From that day on, the class was a stronger group than before.

BUILDING MY INITIATIVE

Initiative grows in the fertile soil of enthusiasm. As adults nurture their own enthusiasm, more initiative develops.

When adults learn and acquire new skills—and get excited and talk about these with friends and colleagues—new initiative develops. Through professional growth we get an ever-replenishing supply of initiative.

Building My Initiative Through Professional Growth

Pop Quiz:
What new skills have I learned recently?

_____
_____
_____

What do I want to learn?

_____

initiative

initiative

ENCOURAGING WORDS ABOUT INITIATIVE

Self-starter   Questioning
Forward-moving   Go-getter
Leader   Energetic
    Mover/Shaker

My Own Words to Inspire My Initiative:

_____

_____

_____

6
PERSEVERANCE
Completing what you start

Successful adults and children are perseverers. They know that if it doesn't work the first time, they have to keep coming back, and back, and back. It may not work even then, but perseverance provides the only possibility that it ever will.

The Problem
Please call back

perseverance

Parents are always telling me how hard it is to reach me. I don't have a phone in my classroom, and the few moments I have between classes provide no time for phone calls. After school, I'm just beat.

perseverance

MegaSkill Moment
Please call back

Parents need to know I do want to talk to them. But they have to understand my tight schedule. In this case, they have to persevere and I have to tell them: "It's OK to keep on calling until you do reach me. Leave messages with work and home numbers at the school office. Don't get discouraged. I promise to call back!"

For certain hours on certain days . . .

perseverance

I'll have a telephone schedule. It might be before school or after dinner. I'll let parents know. When I get a message to return a parent's call, I'll call to set a telephone appointment. When an issue demands longer discussion, we'll set a later time for it or perhaps arrange a conference at school.

perseverance

Sure You're Busy

There seems to be not enough time for almost anything. But, when you really want something done, the old saying is true: "Ask a busy person to do it."

The Problem
Who's up? Who's down?

perseverance

One of the kids in the class got into the habit of shouting out answers, jumping up, seeking attention and getting it.

My approach was to ignore it for a while and then get angry and say, "OK, stop it right now." It would stop until the next day. He and I were both persevering, going through the same routines. I wasn't even aware of what we were doing.

perseverance

MegaSkill Moment
Who's up? Who's down?

My realization: We both needed a way to break this cycle, so he could stop jumping up and I could complete the lesson.

While watching TV one night, I saw a scene that reminded me of what was happening in class. A student kept jumping up out of his chair and the teacher kept pushing him down. It was a parody on what was going on in my own classroom, and I wasn't laughing.

The next day . . .

I surprised the student and the whole class when I said to my young attention-seeker as he bounced out of his seat: "You're just the young man I want to see after class today. We're going to figure out just what's wrong with your chair." Everyone laughed. The student sat down. Maybe the problem is not solved totally, but we're on our way.

perseverance

perseverance

Nag, Nag, Nag

Who says nagging is bad? Today, with everyone so busy or saying they're busy, nagging has become a necessity.

The Problem
It's me again

perseverance

Teachers do a lot of asking, pleading, cajoling, and a lot of calling back. It can become discouraging, especially when we're asking someone for a favor, to donate stuff to the school or to help out in the class. We may feel we're intruding when the call is not returned. The temptation is to stop calling.

perseverance

MegaSkill Moment
It's me again

I was in one of those no-one-ever-calls-me-back moods as I stood in the office of one of my popular and successful friends. She was on the phone and I heard her say and really seem to mean it: "I am so glad you kept after me. I have been meaning to call you back, but got sidetracked. I am so pleased that you did not stand on ceremony waiting for me and instead picked up the phone again."

It was a helpful lesson for this teacher.

I learned . . .

that people often expect me to call back, especially busy people. They don't feel it's an intrusion. Instead, for many, it's a favor. Patience and fortitude still work in this busy world. There is a new saying, "If it's important, they'll call back."

BUILDING MY PERSEVERANCE

Communications experts, whose job it is to put messages across, say that these days it takes eight times of telling the same story before the respondents say, "I've heard of that."

We have to keep remembering how many competing messages are in the air. It takes perseverance to get our message across.

Reminder to Myself:
What are those messages I have to keep saying over and over?

_____

_____

_____

Part Two
Working with Others and Putting it All Together Using MegaSkills

7. Caring: showing concern for others

8. Teamwork: working with others

9. Common Sense: using good judgment

10. Problem Solving: putting what you know and what you can do into action

11. Focus: concentrating with a goal in mind

7
CARING
Showing concern for others

Caring is not just for kids. Every teacher, to do good work, needs to feel personally appreciated.

We care about our students and we need them to care about us, too!

The Problem
Teachers need care, too

caring

I work so hard. Sometimes I feel that no one appreciates all that I do.

caring

MegaSkill Moment
Teachers need care, too

My realization: I have to stop depending so much on whether others appreciate me. I have to find ways to be more aware and admiring of my own work.

I can appreciate my students more when I feel less needy . . . and when I know how to appreciate myself.

I commit myself . . .

to a regular routine of rewarding me. I devote at least one minute each day to telling myself one thing I have done right and giving myself at least three words of encouragement.

BUILDING CARING IN MY CLASSROOM

It's good for students to know the adults in their lives are vulnerable and have needs, just as they do.

Students need to know that adults—including their parents and teachers—need caring.

I'll take some time to share with students some of the ways adults need caring. All those Valentine's Day cards are not just for kids.

Notes to Myself
One way (or more) I will show caring for me:

_____
_____
_____

caring

The Problem
Caring in the classroom

caring

There is a growing harshness in my classroom. I can feel it. I can hear my own voice getting more strident and the students voices get louder and louder.

We seem to be *at* each other more than *with* each other.

MegaSkill Moment
Caring in the classroom

I asked myself: "Would I want to be a student in my own classroom?" And my answer to myself was not sufficiently positive.

I decided . . .

to embark on a modest Caring Campaign for our classroom. I encourage the class to brainstorm with me ways they think of to make our classroom a more caring place. Lowering our voices was one of the first suggestions. Some of the kids even urged the class to bring back the word, "please." We have begun the campaign, and I feel optimistic.

CONNECTING WITH PARENTS

These days much blame and finger pointing are aimed at both teachers and parents. Now, more than ever we, teachers and parents, need to care for one another.

The Problem
Understanding each other

caring

There are students who tell me that I just don't understand. They must think that I was never "young once," that I never had any experiences like theirs.

caring

MegaSkill Moment
Understanding each other

My realization: My students know me only as a teacher. They also need to know me more as a human being. Where did I go to school? What kind of student was I? What do I know now that I wish I had known when I was a kid?

This is not the stuff of deep, dark secrets, nor should it be. Yet, it helps to build rapport and understanding between teachers and students.

I decided:

Without revealing more than kids need to know or want to know, I now tell my students more about my own life . . . focusing on my school days. They get to care more about me and it's a history lesson at the same time.

caring

BUILDING MORE CARING WITHIN MY SCHOOL

caring

Teachers may not say it aloud, but we need attention and recognition. And we don't have to wait for it to come from outside the school or from a supervisor.

I'll take a minute to make a call or send a note to another teacher. Remark on something good they did, something that went right.

Reminder Note:

_____

_____

_____

TEACHER TO TEACHER

We need to find more ways to honor and care for one another. I need to take time to notice what other teachers are doing. These things don't have to be big or grand to be noted and cared about. I'll be as specific as possible when I tell them I appreciate what they did.

MODELING CARING

Most of us live, work, and care in the concentric circles of family, friends, school or job, and community. These are like the circles made by a stone dropped into a pool of water, causing new, ever-widening patterns. Your classroom is a place for you to model the caring skills your students need for the other circles in which they live.

8
TEAMWORK
Working with others

I have to remember to think "collaboration," right from the start.

The Problem
Getting the teaching help I need

teamwork

I'm a new teacher and I get all these good ideas for class activities. My students do the activities, but it's not smooth or systematic. It just doesn't seem to be coming together."

I know I need help, but I am almost afraid to ask.

MegaSkill Moment
Getting the teaching help I need

teamwork

I summoned my courage and went to see the experienced teacher next door.

She said she loves to give advice. She felt flattered. And I felt so much better . . . about myself.

Watching how others work . . .

teamwork

helps me. I keep seeing teamwork everywhere, at home, on TV, in newspapers and in the community—people asking for help and getting help. I decided that if they could do it, I could do it, too!

KIDS ARE ON THE TEAM

Kids can do more than we can imagine. When we enjoy and savor student strengths, they will be more likely to enjoy and respect ours.

The Problem
Getting help from students

teamwork

I overheard some of the students talking about our ugly classroom. I thought I really ought to get this place spruced up, but I don't have time to think about it.

MegaSkill Moment
Getting help from students

teamwork

The kids came up with some great ideas, including putting in a reading corner. They even offered some chairs and pillows from home.

It dawned on me . . .

that I should ask the class how they would make the classroom a more pleasant and comfortable place to work in.

By involving them, I got the help I needed and built my students' sense of teamwork. I am going to ask students for ideas more and more.

teamwork

It Is Crowded in Here

Students bring their whole families into the classroom—even when we don't see them. Let's keep this teamwork going!

The Problem
Sometimes it takes two heads!

At a recent parent-teacher conference, one of my student's parents told me that she felt hopeless and helpless about her child who wouldn't get up in the morning, wouldn't get out of bed to get to school on time.

teamwork

teamwork

MegaSkill Moment
Sometimes it takes two heads!

The mother called today to tell me that my suggestion of getting her child his own alarm clock was working, and she thanked me for my good idea.

I had asked . . .

if I could offer a suggestion and she replied, "Yes!" This mother was so discouraged that it was hard for her to believe that such a simple thing as an alarm clock could work. We became a team!

BUILDING MY TEAMWORK SKILLS

In this complex world, there is a need for more and more teamwork. In many ways, we are already working as teams. At home, it might be teaming to do chores. In school, it might be working together to design a lesson plan or a school event.

Notes to Myself
Here are some ways I currently work as a team member. And here is at least one way that being on a team would make things better for me at school and at home:

_____

_____

_____

Humor: The Twelfth MegaSkill?

Having a sense of humor about ourselves is an essential life skill, perhaps the twelfth MegaSkill. There's a big difference between laughing at ourselves and laughing at others. Laughing at ourselves without tearing ourselves down is a sanity keeper. It's a connector, a bond to other people and their experiences.

9
COMMON SENSE
Using good judgment

*We think, we take charge,
we make a change—when we find that what
we thought was working . . . is not
working any more.*

The Problem
Taking charge of feelings—my own

common sense

I lost my temper in class yesterday. When one of the kids gave an answer that was off the wall, I replied sarcastically, "So, that's your best answer, right?" I was sorry as soon as I uttered the words.

common sense

MegaSkill Moment
Taking charge of feelings—my own

Today, I apologized to the class. I told them that I should have controlled my feelings better and that I would try harder in the future.

I thought overnight about my sarcastic remark, and . . .

I didn't like it. My memory took me back to hearing words very similar to mine from a teacher I once had, who did not apologize afterwards. I knew my teacher had been sorry, but could not bring himself to apologize. I vowed to be different.

common sense

BUILDING GOOD JUDGMENT

Common Sense is knowing when something is *right*. In the fairy tale, *Goldilocks and the Three Bears*, when Goldilocks came to the right food, bed, and chair . . . she just knew.

In the real world, knowing when it's just right or almost right, is a lot harder. Building good judgment takes a lot of practice, for children *and* adults.

The Problem
Taking charge of too much talking—my own

common sense

We often overhear words that hurt, yet help. I heard two of my students saying, "I like her but she talks too much." I felt hurt, especially because these were students I thought really liked my class.

common sense

MegaSkill Moment
Taking charge of too much talking—my own

I said to myself, "Maybe I do talk too much; maybe I do need to listen more." I was offended, but I recognized that these students may be right. I decided not to be defensive.

I brought in a timer:

The idea, good for math and observation skills, was for the class to keep time on how much I talked and how much the class talked.

The kids loved it and we all learned a lot. As for me, I am talking less and listening more.

BUILDING MY COMMON SENSE

Most of us struggle to learn to manage time better. Making lists of what we have to do seems daunting. Yet, I try to list even the small, easy to do tasks, and I put a time frame next to each one.

Jobs (from grading papers to mowing the lawn) will be done by such and such a time and day. That way when I get them done, and check them off my list, I realize a sense of well deserved accomplishment.

Another Idea for Managing My Time:

_____

_____

_____

The Problem
Giving myself time

common sense

One of the students complained bitterly to me yesterday about too much homework, about how boring our class is. I felt really under attack and wanted to lash out with my own sense of frustration.

common sense

MegaSkill Moment
Giving myself time

Instead, I took a deep breath and said, "I want to think about what we are saying. Let's talk about this tomorrow."

I gave myself the time I needed . . .

to compose myself. The old saying, "sleep on it," really helps. I sat down the next day calmly with this student and asked for suggestions on how we can manage the homework that needed to be done and even some ways to make the class more interesting. This was the beginning of many good conversations.

common sense

Encouraging Words About Common Sense

Flexible	Level-headed
Grounded	Responsive
Practical	Reasonable
Intuitive	Savvy

My Own Words That Describe My Common Sense:

_____

_____

_____

THE JEWEL OF COMMON SENSE

Don't pay attention to anyone who says, "It's *just* common sense," as though it's nothing much because everyone knows it. Common sense is one of the riches that many, if not most, teachers are blessed with. That word "just" can't tarnish the value of this MegaSkill. Our goal is to use common sense and use it proudly.

People Common Sense

Another aspect of common sense can be called "people common sense." It involves showing concern for others, but it also means seeing things from other points of view, i.e., putting ourselves, as best we can, in other people's shoes.

10
PROBLEM SOLVING
Putting what you know and what you can do into action

Expect problems. They come with the territory. It wouldn't be teaching without them.

The Problem
When the talking has to stop

One of the most helpful parents, when she comes to see me or work with the class, just can't seem to stop talking. It's personal stuff, not school-related.

I don't want to be rude, but when she goes on and on, I feel like just leaving the room.

problem solving

MegaSkill Moment
When the talking has to stop

problem solving

Today, I figured out how to cut down on the talking and still not hurt her feelings. I told her how every minute in class counts and how valuable she is to the kids. "So, let's get to it and make sure the kids get the most of your valuable help."

I put myself in her shoes:

How would I want someone to treat me if and when I was taking up so much time? So, I listened to the words I would say in my head before I said them aloud. They sounded fine to me and so I used them . . . and they sounded fine to her, too.

SMALL PROBLEMS, BIG TROUBLE

Problems don't have to be big to cause trouble. Even the smallest pebble in a shoe irritates the foot.

We face problems every day that involve difficult people and troublesome situations. Fortunately, we can solve most of theses problems by using our MegaSkills.

The Problem
When the griping had to stop

Report cards came out yesterday. Today two of my students came in to complain about their grades. They said I was unfair and went on and on. I felt really uncomfortable, because I pride myself on being fair.

problem solving

MegaSkill Moment
When the griping had to stop

problem solving

After being labeled "unfair," the kids told me after our meeting that I really was fair. The students calmed down and I, especially, felt a lot better.

I save . . .

problem solving

many of my class's papers and keep a file of each student's work. I dug into these portfolios, came up with the papers and showed the kids how I arrived at their grades. Once they saw their own work, they admitted that their grades were fair. We moved on to how they could improve their grades for the next marking period. All in all, it was a positive, productive meeting.

BUILDING MY PROBLEM SOLVING

To be sure, there are all kinds of problems, some much more scary than others, life-or-death ones versus the nagging glitches of everyday life.

Working on problems that lend themselves to solutions helps me to have a sense of personal achievement. I get that surge of satisfaction when I can, for example, figure out a shortcut to get to school, discover a way to cut down on monthly bills, or get the video recorder to actually record.

Notes to Myself About a Problem Solved, or To Be Solved

_____

_____

_____

The Problem
When the cheating had to stop

problem solving

Today, I caught one of my better students cheating in class. He was looking at another student's paper and very obviously copying the answers. I tapped the student on the shoulder and asked him to stay to talk with me after class.

MegaSkill Moment
When the cheating had to stop

problem solving

This student, for the first time, asked me for extra help and admitted that he was troubled with this part of the schoolwork. He had never asked for help before and had always put on a great show of knowing all the answers.

When I called the student aside, . . .

without recrimination, I said that there was no reason to cheat, ever. "You can come to me for extra help whenever you need it," I confided. He said that he didn't want me to think that he wasn't smart. I replied that the smart person, adult or child, knows when to ask for help.

problem solving

ENCOURAGING WORDS ABOUT PROBLEM SOLVING

Nuts and Bolts	Analytical
Big Picture	Sensible
Proactive	Deductive
Uses Knowledge	

Words That Describe My Problem Solving:

_____

_____

_____

11
FOCUS
Concentrating with a goal in mind

*Paying attention is harder than ever,
when everything seems to be clamoring
for my attention all at once.*

The Problem
Getting ready to focus

There is so much more to remember. I feel as if I spend half my day forgetting things. Hunting for keys, looking for eyeglasses, searching for important papers—it's a struggle just to keep together the things I need.

focus

MegaSkill Moment
Getting Ready To Focus

My realization: A lot of this forgetting is connected to stress. My stress gets reduced when I consciously set aside places for everything I really need. Then I can be sure that what I need will be where I expect to find it.

I use a strategy . . .

focus

that lets me use my head, but doesn't require me to remember everything. I set up a structure that lets me make better use of my environment. My keys always go on a certain hook. In a blue file, go the papers I need for Monday. In that red file, go the papers I need for Tuesday, and so on.

Everyone needs to come up with a personal strategy. The simpler the better. I can let those hooks and colored files do a lot of the remembering for me.

WHEN MORE IS NOT BETTER

The operative word today is *more*—more information, more to do, more of just about everything, except time. How can you handle it all? You don't have to. Focus on what you *can* accomplish.

The Problem
Coping, but with a plan

The materials, the reports, the papers are pouring in from everywhere. I feel inundated. Often, I wish I could just throw all the papers away.

focus

MegaSkill Moment
Coping, but with a plan

focus

I set a goal of getting over this paper mountain, but first I needed a plan. I call it— One Pile at a Time. Right from the start I excused myself of the obligation of having to read everything from cover to cover. My objective was to handle the really important stuff immediately.

I went through the mounds of material and . . .

made three piles. **Pile 1:** Do it now! **Pile 2:** Material that was important but could wait. **Pile 3:** Material that either went into the wastebasket or could wait quite a while.

This made me feel better right away. Pile 1 did not intimidate and Pile 2 began to look inviting. Pile 3 began to look more like recreational reading, to be saved for a treat.

focus

COPING WITH THE BIG STUFF

All this information flooding in, it swirls and swirls about me.

It's like being caught in a storm But I can cope. I can muster the strength to do the little things and bigger things it takes to weather the storm. I try to break the bigger things down into smaller chunks. Then massive tasks become just more small stuff.

The Problem
Moving forward: One step at a time

focus

My plans got fouled up again. I'd planned to spend a full day getting my classroom into shape. Now, I've been called to a meeting outside the school. When will I ever get to do what I have to do?

MegaSkill Moment
Moving forward: One step at a time

focus

I can see progress. It's almost a miracle! I thought I needed a long, complete block of time to arrange my classroom. It might have been easier that way, but I managed to do it in little pieces of time, over a two-week period. I identified my goal, made a step-by-step plan and stuck to it.

When I realized I may never have the big piece of time I had hoped for, . . .

focus

I focused my mind on incremental ways I could get the job done. On Monday, I would do the class files; on Tuesday, I would do the bookcases; on Wednesday, the kids would work with me on the bulletin boards, and so on. The progress is slower. It's one step at a time, but I'm getting to my goal.

BUILDING MY FOCUS

Reminders to Me:

Name an upcoming personal goal:

_____

Identify a first step:

_____

Measure my progress:

_____

_____

The special strength of focus as a MegaSkill is that it connects so well to meeting goals. Goal setting has the remarkable ability to keep our minds and our thinking centered. When we work toward a goal, measuring our progress along the way, we use all of our MegaSkills more and feel more productive, more involved.

Part Three
Grading Ourselves

My MegaSkills Report Card

About the Author

About MegaSkills and the Home and School Institute

Further Reading from the NEA Professional Library

12
My MegaSkills Report Card
One way of giving ourselves the credit we deserve

Grading Ourselves
My MegaSkills® Report Card

report card

Here are some ways to help us measure our progress on the Road to MegaSkills. It is a journey—and the important point is to never give up, neither on the job nor at home.

The Report Card, which begins on the next page, lists but a few of the ways we show our MegaSkills. Add to this list. Keep asking: What else do I do?

My MegaSkills Report Card

My MegaSkills	Frequently Observed	Sometimes Observed	Needs Work
Confidence: • Take pride in my own achievement. • Avoid putting down others. • Show sense of own strengths and areas to be improved. •			
Motivation: • Approach daily challenges with positive attitudes. • Indicate readiness to know more and do more. •			
Effort: • Demonstrate self-discipline to manage time and tasks. • Complete work consistently and carefully. •			
Responsibility: • Show ability to organize self and work. • Remember to do what is needed to get jobs done. • Work to do the right thing. •			

report card

My MegaSkills Report Card

My MegaSkills	Frequently Observed	Sometimes Observed	Needs Work
Initiative: • Come up with new ideas; assume leadership roles. • Show understanding of what needs to be done and how to accomplish those tasks. • • •			
Perseverance: • Show ability to stick with an assignment or project to completion. • Tolerate frustration when working through problems. • • •			
Caring: • Show kindness, concern, and offer praise to others. • Demonstrate consideration, ability to share and be helpful to others. • • •			

report card

My MegaSkills Report Card

My MegaSkills	Frequently Observed	Sometimes Observed	Needs Work
Teamwork: • Work cooperatively with others. • Provide and take feedback and criticism. •			
Common Sense: • Know how to prevent and solve problem situations. • Predict what may happen as a result of personal behaviors and attitudes. •			
Problem Solving: • Show ability and readiness to tackle new situations. • Seek innovative and diverse solutions to problems. •			
Focus: • Show ability to set personal goals, maintain direction, and avoid distraction. • Show commitment to meet goals, handle stress, and control emotions. •			

report card

AND REMEMBER...

Every day is a new start.

> Every day is the first day of school.

As an adult, I continue to grow and learn.

> Even "grown-ups" grow new brain cells...

I must nurture myself so that I can continue to grow and to educate.

Creating My Own Idea Sparkers

_____

_____

_____

An "end" is always a new beginning . . .

About the Author

Dorothy Rich, Ed.D., is founder and president of the nonprofit Home and School Institute (HSI) based in Washington, DC. An acclaimed expert in family educational involvement, she is the author of the original MegaSkills publications and is the developer of the MegaSkills training programs used by over three thousand schools across the United States and abroad. In her lifetime of work in the field, she has focused on helping families and educators team together to build achievement for school and beyond.

Dr. Rich's work has received the A+ for Breaking the Mold Award from the US Department of Education as well as recognition from the MacArthur Foundation and other distinguished foundations. Her work has been researched, tested, and found to be effective in raising student achievement, decreasing discipline problems, increasing homework time, and decreasing time spent watching TV. Her work has been featured in *The Washington Post*, *The New York Times*, *The Los Angeles Times*, *NBC's Today Show*, *Education Week*, *USA Today*, *Good Morning America*, and *Newsweek*.

About MegaSkills and the Home and School Institute

The major focus of the nonprofit Home and School Institute (HSI), with its MegaSkills Education Center, is to build children's achievement in school and beyond. With programs beginning in 1972, HSI, founded by Dr. Dorothy Rich, has developed systematic training and materials for teachers to use with families in parent involvement programs and with students directly in the classroom.

MegaSkills Leader Training Workshops: The MegaSkills Education Center under the leadership of Harriett Stonehill, Director, trains and certifies MegaSkills leaders to conduct parent workshops. This program, now in 48 states and available in Spanish, is sponsored by schools, business, and community organizations.

MegaSkills Essentials for the Classroom: This program trains teachers/leaders to provide MegaSkills activities in academics, character development and MegaSkills attitudes and behaviors.

Tested results from MegaSkills Programs:
- Higher achievement scores
- Higher attendance rates
- Fewer school discipline problems
- Increased homework time
- Increased participation by all families in children's education

HSI has worked for many years with NEA members nationally. HSI is a 501 (c)(3) organization supported by foundations, government grants, and individual contributions.

Home and School Institute Publications

While HSI training materials, in English and Spanish, are available only through the MegaSkills training program, HSI has developed related publications to reach a wider public.

MegaSkills®: Building Children's Achievement for the Information Age. Expanded Edition. Activities to teach confidence, motivation, effort, responsibility, initiative, perseverance, caring, teamwork, common sense, problem solving and focus. This edition has new sections on technology and employabilities. (Houghton Mifflin)

What Do We Say? What Do We Do? Vital Solutions for Children's Educational Success This new book uses MegaSkills to solve natural stresses and frustrations of the home/school relationship. Each chapter provides situations and activities using actual words children say and suggests parent responses when wrenching everyday problems come home from school. (Tor/Forge)

Survival Guide for Today's Parents: Book and Audiocassettes
Dozens of tested, easy activities for home use.

The New MegaSkills Bond
Practical strategies to build partnerships with families and the community.

**MegaSkills Education Center of the
Home and School Institute**
1500 Massachusetts Ave., NW Washington, DC 20005
(202) 466-3633 Fax: (202) 833-1400
Web: www.MegaSkillsHSI.org

Further Reading from the NEA Professional Library

The NEA Professional Library is the nation's leading publisher devoted exclusively to providing professional development materials for educators. Showcasing our more than 200 books and videos, the NEA Professional Library catalog can be your one-stop source for:
- innovative products for new teachers,
- practical strategies that can inspire quality in your school,
- teacher-written books that explore the latest trends and provide practical applications for ground-breaking research in education, and
- video programs that spotlight teaching and learning innovations developed by NEA members.

The NEA Professional Library is a not-for-profit service financed solely by the sale of books and other professional development materials to the education community.

Want to read more by Dorothy Rich? Try:

Learning & Working: Basics For Children
by Dorothy Rich
This unique school-to-work publication helps middle school (and younger) students begin to develop the skills they need to succeed in the work world.
#2002-2-00-MM, Non-members $15.95, NEA Members $11.95

NEA Professional Library, P.O. Box 2035,
Annapolis Junction, MD 20701-2035
800-229-4200

More reading for beginning teachers:

The First Year Teacher: Teaching with Confidence (K-8)
by Karen Bosch & Katharine Kersey
The ultimate first-year teacher's handbook.
#1862-1-00-MM, Non-members $18.95, NEA Members $14.95

Countdown to the First Day of School: A 60-Day Get-Ready Checklist
by Leo Schell & Paul Burden
A must-have checklist for every beginning elementary teacher.
#2150-9-00-MM, Non-members $4.95, NEA Members $4.50

Bright Ideas: A Pocket Mentor for Beginning Teachers
by Mary Clement
This checklist reveals the secrets of surviving the first year of teaching.
#2153-3-00-MM, Non-members $4.95, NEA Members $4.50

Pitfalls and Potholes: A Checklist for Avoiding Common Mistakes of Beginning Teachers
by Barbara A. Murray and Kenneth T. Murray
This bestseller makes a perfect gift for new teachers.
#2151-7-00-MM, Non-members $4.95, NEA Members $4.50

NEA Professional Library, P.O. Box 2035,
Annapolis Junction, MD 20701-2035
800-229-4200

More reading from Teacher-to-Teacher Books
Published by the NEA Professional Library

The 13 innovative books listed below are written by teachers. Inside each book you will find several candid stories of how teachers across the country are tackling specific school change challenges. They take you step by step through a description of what worked and didn't work. In addition, important ideas and helpful shortcuts are presented in reproducible, user-friendly diagrams, checklists, and tables. Each book costs $9.95 for NEA members and $12.95 for non-members

Beyond Textbooks: Hands-On Learning.
96pp. 1995. (2906-2-00-MM)
Building Parent Partnerships.
96pp. 1996. (2911-9-00-MM)
How to Get Grants and Free Stuff.
96pp. 1998 (2914-3-00-MM)
Innovative Discipline.
96pp. 1994. (2904-6-00-MM)
Integrated Thematic Teaching.
96pp. 1996. (2909-7-00-MM)
Multi-Age Classrooms.
96pp. 1995. (2907-0-00-MM)
Multiple Intelligences.
96pp. 1996. (2910-0-00-MM)
Peer Support: Teachers Mentoring Teachers.
96pp. 1998 (2913-5-00-MM)
School-Based Change.
96pp. 1994. (2905-4-00-MM)
Student Portfolios.
96pp. 1993. (2901-1-00-MM)
Technology for Diverse Learners.
96pp. 1997. (2908-9-00-MM)
Time Strategies: Block Scheduling and Beyond.
96pp. 1994. (2902-X-00-MM)
Toward Inclusive Classrooms.
96pp. 1994. (2903-8-00-MM)

NEA Professional Library, P.O. Box 2035,
Annapolis Junction, MD 20701-2035
800-229-4200